A Lovely Place

Lazaro's Story

A Lovely Place

Lazaro's Story

Translated by David Stewart, M.D.
Foreword by Dr. Dennis F. Kinlaw

fap

francis asbury press

Scripture quotations are from The King James Version
Editor: Mark Royster
Layout: Vicki New

Cover art: MAFA PENTECOST
Used by permission
All rights reserved
Vie de Jesus MAFA
24 rue du Marechal Joffre
F-7800 VERSAILLES
www.jesusmafa.com

Copyright © 2009
ISBN: 978-0-915143-13-9

Published by
The Francis Asbury Society
PO Box 7, Wilmore, KY 40390-0007
859-858-4222
FrancisAsb@aol.com
www.francisasburysociety.com

Introduction

We are indebted to the late David Stewart, M.D. for preserving the amazing testimony you are about to read.

Following World War II, David and his wife, Laura, together with George and Willouise Luce, pioneered the medical work of the World Gospel Mission at Murore, Burundi. They began under canvas, operating out of a surplus Mobile Army Surgical Hospital. With remarkable foresight and ingenuity George Luce built the permanent facility, making use of a nearby stream to provide both water and hydro-electricity. The whole project was engineered from the ground up with appropriate technology for sustainable service. Over the next fifteen years Murore became a thriving place of healing, training and evangelistic outreach.

In 1962 David Stewart returned home to the U.S. where he practiced psychiatry in Louisville, Kentucky. He remained actively involved in missions until his death in 1989, consulting with various mission boards on mental health and medical concerns. A committed member of the Christian Medical and Dental Associations, David designed and led the first Medical Education International conferences in Africa and Southeast Asia. Today these traveling teams of highly-qualified teaching faculty continue to keep medical missionaries professionally current and spiritually refreshed while they serve far from the resources of home.

After Murore Hospital was completed, George Luce joined his brothers, Joseph and Albert, Jr., at the helm of the family bus manufacturing business, The Blue Bird Body Company of Ft. Valley, Georgia. He never lost his heart for missions or his commitment to the message contained in this story. The remarkable success of Bluebird provided funding for countless mission projects around the world during his lifetime. Today the Luce family remains a quiet but potent force in Christian philanthropy.

Following its independence from Belgian colonial rule, Burundi experienced a succession of flawed governments and tragic episodes of ethnic violence. Missionary and humanitarian efforts were hampered and development stalled. World Gospel Mission was eventually forced to close its work in Burundi and redeploy their personnel to other fields.

For many years it was difficult to know what became of the Murore Station. In 1985, through a series of unlikely connections, I was able to catch a ride from Bujumbura to Murore in a United Nations Land-Cruiser. At that time only U.N. vehicles could pass freely through the numerous military checkpoints along the way. What I found was discouraging, but not surprising. The hospital had been reduced to a small clinic dispensing contraceptives and a random assortment of drugs donated by various aid organizations. One lone medical student was on hand fulfilling his obligation to the government with temporary service at this remote outpost. He had a small Honda generator to provide light for nighttime emergencies but not much else. The beds and all the equipment were gone. The church and school were empty.

Those solid brick buildings stand silent now, but the testimony of Lazaro Nitunga will always be part of the remaining fruit of the Murore mission. Lazaro's life and witness demonstrate how the Spirit of God often works so beautifully on the "edges" of what we consider most important.

In reprinting Lazaro's message we hope it will stir your heart with renewed hope and hunger for the transforming work of the Holy Spirit. Two thousand years ago the same Spirit launched a group of frightened men into bold and joyful witness in a hostile world. Wherever the Holy Spirit moves, the love of God begins to take over in life-changing and world-changing ways. He is still moving today.

Mark Royster
Advent 2008

Foreword

by Dennis F. Kinlaw

Recently I was given a copy of *Lazaro's Story* and found myself instantly captivated. It was my privilege to know George Luce and David Stewart personally and to be familiar with their work in Burundi. Thus reading *Lazaro's Story* was like a visit with treasured friends.

As I read further I found a deeper interest. The unique expressions that come through in the English translation of Lazaro's words added to my fascination. It was obviously a story from another culture. Yet I found in the profound simplicity and purity of his witness an inescapable appeal, in spite of the differences of the syntax and vocabulary. Who would not be charmed by his description of the promise in the center of God's will: "You shall arrive at a very lovely place, and you shall not ever desire greatly to come out from that place"?

I found myself wondering what Jesus' own disciples would think if they were to be given a copy of *Lazaro's Story*. I could almost hear Peter say: "Why, his story is like ours! That's the way it was for us. There were six years between Lazaro's beginning to follow Christ and his being filled with the Holy Spirit; for us it was only a bit over three years; but his story and ours are essentially the same." And I could imagine John's reply: "Yes! When the Spirit came to us in fullness we received that same kind of overflowing love for Christ. He filled us and freed us from the fear and self-interest that had muddied our discipleship and clouded our witness. The Spirit that released us to be wholly Christ's did the same thing for Lazaro."

I then thought back to my younger days when I was influenced by the little book by the president of Wheaton College, Dr. V. Raymond Edman, *They Found the Secret*. Dr. Edman had himself been influenced by a volume by J. Gilchrist Lawson, *Deeper Experiences of Famous Christians*. I remembered the testimonies I heard from evangelical leaders in those days. They consistently described an experience of the Holy Spirit after their conversion. Unlike so many testimonies today, their emphasis was not upon empowering gifts to make them famous, but a humbling that cleansed them of self-will, so that the passion of their lives was no longer ministerial success but faithful submission to Christ no matter what it might involve.

I recalled with ringing clarity the witness of a dear friend and nationally-known leader. "Dennis," he said, "I was the son of a Baptist preacher. I found Christ as my savior during my high school days. I attended Wheaton College and then went to UCLA for doctoral studies. My fiancé sent me a copy of Oswald Chambers' *My Utmost for His Highest*. Chambers found me out, and God brought me to a surrender so total, so complete that it has never had to be done over again."

My friend is now in the multitude around God's throne, but, if he were here, I think he would say, "Dennis, *Lazaro's Story* is my story, too. And it needs to be every Christian's story." That is why we felt this should be published. Is it your story? It can be.

Original Foreword
by
David Stewart, M.D.
Murore 1955

    The message contained in the following pages deserves your attention. We believe it to be one of the most unusual things you have ever read. But let us tell you about it.

    The spring of 1949 found the medical program at Murore in great need. No such program can exist without African clinical workers and ours was a young mission, lacking in trained national staff. We had depended heavily on one young man but he slipped into temptation and failed us painfully. In desperation we called on other, older missions for help. Lazaro Nitunga, of a distant Church of England mission, felt called to accept. For him this was a difficult matter as it meant moving far from home, family and friends.

When he came to us he had gone to his mission school for five years and had worked about two years in their hospital. He was perhaps eighteen years of age, tall and strong. With hardly an effort he slipped into his new life with us, easily shouldering new and greater responsibilities. It quickly became apparent that he was no ordinary young man. His medical aptitude grew swiftly along with his zeal for Christ. Most important of all he avoided that trap of pride. Since coming to us he has married a local girl, has two children, and is continuing in the work.

The pages ahead contain a sermon he wrote. A few days previous he had delivered it in our Sunday worship service. Miss Isabel Luce was present, and as I translated it to her, she began to glow. It was at her request that he put the sermon on paper and its publication is dedicated to her memory. Remember, it was written in the language of the Batutsi people, then translated into English as directly as possible, and this literal translation is presented here.

My Testimony

Come now, and let us reason together, saith the Lord: though your sins be as scarlet, they shall be white as snow."
-Isaiah 1:18

I am happy to speak on this word because I speak what I saw in my heart, not doubting. I am not able to speak everything well but those who know will understand.

We speak this sanctification word in many ways — we say: to be "made white" (Isaiah 1:18), to be "filled with the Holy Spirit," the "second blessing," to be "baptized in the Holy Spirit and in fire." But everything says one thing. That thing is this: It is to find the power of the Holy Spirit to make us able to testify for Jesus; we have finished our poverty, and we have finished fear (Acts 1:8). Also our eyes are made open and we see well the work of God. These words concerning sanctification are not words for those who are not yet saved, they are words for those who have come out from death and have arrived at life.

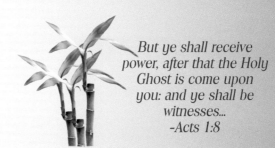

But ye shall receive power, after that the Holy Ghost is come upon you: and ye shall be witnesses...
-Acts 1:8

Some when saved only a short time receive that second blessing; others wait a long time. But saved ones who desire greatly to demonstrate the light of the One who redeems us among those who are not saved must find that second blessing.

THE TWELVE SENT ONES

Stop and let us think of those who began the holy church. We know that Jesus came to light a fire in the world and the fire began to grasp hold of the twelve. Or we would say: Jesus was a large plant and all of us branches, but there are twelve big branches, and from these large ones we have come forth. These people were people as we are. They did not know very much wisdom; they were men of worldly things. These things helped them in their bodies but they had not yet received that thing which surpasses all things of the world, which gives the heart peace: He is Jesus.

I am come that they might have life, and that they might have it more abundantly.
-John 10:10

Therefore, King Jesus found them as they were in among their things. Some were fishermen, others were tax gatherers, but then He called them. Also He did not tell them many words or strong words, but He told them two things only.

One was, "Follow me." The other was, "I will make you to be those who fish for men." These were not words to make them leave their riches. But because they were made to see by Jesus that it was of a great price which surpassed everything, they followed Him. These people were shown Christ completely and He surpassed for them all their riches.

Also, now all of the time they went about with Him and they loved Him much. They knew that it was He who was the word of life which does not come to an end (John 6:68). Also, they knew that it was He, Christ, the Son of the living God (Matt. 16:16). So those things show us that they loved Him, and they did not want to be separated from Him.

But King Jesus, in the time when He was near to be crucified, showed them that they were still small in the path of God. He told them that He would send One to them but they did not understand at that time, because they did not know that there was another thing necessary for them. They were happy to be together with their King only. But Jesus knew their little strength. He knew that the things of the world were still in their eyes. They were still headed for the important things of this world; they were still being conquered by anger and covetousness.

So the Lord Jesus, that night when they took Him to be crucified, He showed the disciples their little strength. He said, "All of you this night, will be thrown by the things that cause men to fall."

And so after a little time only, that little strength showed itself plainly. When they had seen their King taken hold of, all of them fled. An important thing which conquered them was fear. Peter wanted to follow Him, but when this happened, he was afraid. He lied. He said, "I do not know this one of whom you speak."

Now when Jesus had finished to arise, He continued to consider their little strength. He found them in the house with the door closed and they had much fear. They were afraid of the Jews. They did not have the strength to stand up in front of the Jews. Then one day they went back to fishing. Peter said, "I go to fish." Others said, "We will go along." These things show that they still did not have their eyes open that they should see completely the work of God.

So thus King Jesus saw that they were not able to begin the work of God, that of testifying to His resurrection. For that reason He prevented them from leaving Jerusalem.

And, being assembled together with them, He commanded them that they should not depart from Jerusalem, but wait for the promise of the Father, which, saith he, ye have heard of me. For John truly baptized with water; but ye shall be baptized with the Holy Ghost not many days hence.
-Acts 1:4-5

So in their meeting He forbade them that they leave Jerusalem but He said, "Wait for the promise of the Father which you have heard from me. John caused to baptize with water, but you in these days shall be baptized with the Holy Spirit" (Acts 1:4-5). He prevented them from beginning the Work of God in order that they wait for that One who speaks for us.

But they did not know that they would be changed when that One who speaks for us had finished to come. Then Jesus showed them completely what they would be like when they had finished to receive that One who speaks for us. He said, "You shall have power when the Holy Spirit comes upon you, you shall be witnesses to testify of me, in Jerusalem and in all Judea and in Samaria to reach out to the ends of the earth" (Acts 1:8). When they heard this they stayed there and they prayed and waited.

Then on that day set by God, it was then they saw what was promised them, what was a miracle of God (Acts 2:1). The multitude also saw this event and it surprised everybody who was there.

And when the day of Pentecost was fully come, they were all with one accord in one place. And suddenly there came a sound from heaven as of a rushing mighty wind, and it filled all the house where they were sitting. And there appeared unto them cloven tongues like as of fire, and it sat upon each of them. And they were all filled with the Holy Ghost.
-Acts 2:1-4

THE CHANGE IN THE MEN

They were changed into completely other people. Fear was ended. Peter, that one who feared a little girl, it was he who stood in the midst of the great crowd of Jews and testified that Jesus arose from the dead (Acts 2:14-36). Oh, no, they didn't continue to fear, not once, in front of the people who saw them, and these people marveled at the power which they had finished to receive. The people saw the end of fear in Peter and John. Also they saw that they were not educated, that they were not people of wisdom, but they knew that they had been with Jesus (Acts 4:13).

THE PROMISE IS OURS!

When Peter had finished to speak what was sent (the Gospel), people repented. But he told them that they should receive a Gift, the Holy Spirit (Acts 2:37-39). When he had finished speaking he said, "The promise is for you and for your children." Also he said, "And all that are afar off, they shall be called by our Lord God."

All these who are far off means, "All of those of other tribes." All of us, we were far away, but the promise is ours. All those who have received this Gift, we witness to it. Also for all those who have not yet received, the promise is theirs. God does not change or contradict what He has said.

MY SALVATION

I want to testify to what I saw in my life, the way I was saved and the manner in which I found holiness of heart. I was saved in 1939. I was a child and I was in school. I was a child praised by my parents and by my teachers. Also the word of God had finished to enter into my heart, telling me that I was not yet saved and that I would go to the Fire That Does Not Finish. But I thought about it.

I said, "Tell me, I have not done any big sin and my parents and my teachers always praise me. Am I not a good child? Tell me, I shall be saved from what?"

But the voice of God always continually spoke in my heart telling me, "No matter how you are praised, you are in the bonds of Satan. Also you are blind and you know it. You have a heavy burden."

But my good time arrived. In September of 1939, I saw the cross in my heart, and I discovered that good Person, that no sin He did, that He was crucified on the cross because of me. But at first I did not accept it, as I was in trouble for my sins, but it was made known to me, and that voice continued stronger and stronger to speak in my heart, telling me that I would die a bad death if I did not find what would save me from my sins. So when that voice finished to lift up my many sins before me, I felt that there was a great burden. I could not find what would take my burden off in order that I might rest, and I cried. While I was thus still confused, it was then that the cross was revealed to me. He who was crucified there was one of great mercy. Thus when I finally saw the cross, that burden left me and I was left with much peace.

Also, it surprised me because I saw a thing I had not seen before in my life. Thus when I found that salvation, I knew that I was a child of God, also that my name was written in the book of life. Also I gave my testimony among the children with whom I associated, also among those with whom I learned in school. Also at home and in the village I showed them what I had found which I did not have before. Also I told them that even though they praised me, I was not saved before.

In the last day, that great day of the feast, Jesus stood and cried, saying, If any man thirst, let him come unto me, and drink. He that believeth on me, as the scripture hath said, out of his belly shall flow rivers of living water.
-John 7:37-38

MY SANCTIFICATION

Thus for some time I went on in that life and I was happy in what I found; it was that life which does not end. Also in that time I saw Satan had much zeal to put me back into sin. Also I was afraid that he would conquer, because I felt that I did not have strength to stand and fight well. But in that time I did not yet know that there was another thing necessary to receive, which would make me able to conquer very much. I did not know that there was another thing to surpass what I had found. I did not know that there was a second blessing.

What troubled me in my heart was that I was defeated often. I desired greatly to conquer, but I found that I was conquered. There was sin in me which I did not know. Also what continued more and more to rule was fear. I remembered that it brought me into sin of telling lies, and to surpass that it prevented me from witnessing for my Lord. I did not fear to testify before the children and small groups (when there were not very many). Among important people, big chiefs or sub-chiefs, or grownups of the Batutsi, I feared to testify. When I arrived among them I was afraid and kept quiet. I did not yet have those rivers of life of which Jesus spoke in John 7:37-39.

I had much need completely in my heart. I felt that I was saved, and also others knew that I was saved, because they saw the signs. But I realized that I was a needy one completely. Also others saw that I had need. But I did not know what I must do in order that I find the way to lose my great need. I was troubled when I saw that others conquered and that their needs were satisfied. I still desired greatly to conquer but I did not know the path by which to conquer.

You shall arrive at a very lovely place, and you shall not ever desire greatly to come out from that place.

One time a brother in the church had his needs satisfied. He said in a great voice, "You, my brethren, saved ones, persevere to go forward beyond. You shall arrive at a very lovely place, and you shall not ever desire greatly to come out from that place."

So when I heard these words I asked myself, "Is there another nice place where I will arrive except where I have come to?" But I continued to meditate, "There is! It is true because others have arrived there. Now they are satisfied and they have lost their need."

I stayed in that life six whole years. I think that in those years not much work did I do to serve my Lord. I wanted to serve Him, but I lacked the power to conquer.

Then one time in a good year of God, He looked into my need. I felt the need of my heart, and the hunger and thirst grew increasingly more and more. Also I looked more and more at others to see the manner that they were satisfied and had a life which conquers. And I began to put my need before God and prayed with great fervor. I did not receive at that time I began to pray, but even though I did not receive at that time, I did not stop praying.

I persevered much, and I discovered that word, "Ask and ye shall receive, knock and it shall be opened unto you." Also I discovered that Jesus told those sent ones, "Wait for the promise of the Father." So I continued to pray, believing. Also I began to be shown sins I did not know of which were in me. Also in myself I heard a voice saying, "I was brought that they might have life and that they find life and running over." Then I felt that power of the Holy Spirit burned up all of the sins of the past, which had conquered me. I felt that need met. I felt the rivers of life pouring into me.

At that time I began to be shown the Book of God, entirely new, and testimonies of the things of Jesus did not trouble me, because the things of God filled my heart, and afterwards they spilled out and flowed to others. Now and then this filled me while I was sleeping and I would awake and tell those with me about it. Also in the work I was in, in the dispensary, it spilled out; when I went to teach the sick I did not get tired because I testified to what Jesus worked in my heart. The sick and the well saw what Jesus worked in that time, because this was not something that could be hidden. Also the work of God began to reveal itself to me in a new way.

MY CALL TO SERVICE

I was shown the lost, and it became a burden to me. Often I remembered that there were those for whom Christ died who were not yet saved. These things prevented me from sleeping. I left my sleep and prayed for the lost ones. Also as I prayed more and more for the lost ones, in this way I saw the blessings of the Lord which descended on me as a river, that very time while I was praying. Also as I heard the things of God made known to me, thus I told them more and more to the young and old. And as I told them, at the very time when I was speaking, I felt that again this flowed over me as a river. As my eyes were made to see, I understood the need of others and I prayed for them. Thus I felt that I must do everything by that Light that Jesus lighted in the earth.

In that year that I received these things, I was working in the dispensary but during my time to rest I did not go home to please myself as I was used to doing. What I found forced me to go to the hills to tell others of the power which is in Jesus, and it was thus that I began to give myself. I sold myself to my King, that even though He call me to go very far I would go because of the price He gave for me on the cross. At first I did not go to another country because I liked my own very much.

But in 1950 I heard the voice of God calling me to go to serve God elsewhere. I had not heard that voice in other years, but I was expecting it to come for I had finished to give myself. And when I had heard it I did not fear, even though it was a country I did not know. I believed that I would meet with troubles. Also my friends feared that I would find much to trouble me. But I set my goal to demonstrate and to tell others what Jesus had done for me. I did not look forward to good or bad which I would meet in my temporal life. What was in my life, it was what led me. I was not driving myself.

BUT WE CANNOT REST

That good blessing which I received has remained with me until now. And it comforts my heart and makes it rest. Sometimes I feel that it is not great, I feel little strength, but deep in my heart is that Holy Spirit whom I found: He is within.

Paul wrote Timothy saying, "For this reason I remind you that thou stir up the Gift of God which is in you." This shows that there are things that are able to cover that good gift of God, that it burns dimly. So we must always remember to stir it up. If we accept the Holy Spirit to rule our hearts, He will make us clean. He will remain with us every day. He will make us able to do the things which are difficult for us, or which "down" us.

Saved ones on this earth, we are in a battle! But if the Holy Spirit rules us, we shall conquer because it is He who will conquer. Also especially the battle of the body is hard, because we fight with ourselves. But if we have given ourselves to the Holy Spirit and He reigns in us, our old nature will move out and the Holy Spirit will conquer us.

WHAT WE MUST DO TO KEEP WHAT WE HAVE BEEN GIVEN

That gift of sanctification is a good gift, and we have received it because of the grace of God. For that reason we must guard holiness in our hearts. We must shepherd well this pearl of great price. He who is tainted by this world or by the things of the body, hears and feels that the Holy Spirit calls him to repent. If he waits, he will have lost that holiness. If we want to retain that experience we must not wait or be tardy at what the Holy Spirit says. I want to say four things which are able to help us to hold that holiness of heart. It is not to say that it is these things only that we must do to remain in a holy place. There are others in the Word of God, but if we are in these we know that we are in holiness of heart.

1) Pray without ceasing.

We must pray every day and at all times, in order that we conquer the bad spirit. It is not to pray along with others only . . . but we must get in a solitary place with God, and we tell Him everything as a parent, all those things which trouble our minds and our hearts.

And it is not that only. We must pray in our hearts, when we are standing, when we are chatting with others, when we are traveling in the path, we must with every breath think of the things of God, that our hearts look to heaven. Thus we conquer the bad spirits of Satan.

2) Read the Word of God daily.

While we are reading the Word of God, we are eating the food of life. For that reason we must not miss to read the Word of God. If we miss reading we will be hungry. Also when we read, we take out what we can feed to others.

3) Obey the Holy Spirit.

And the very God of peace sanctify you wholly; and I pray God your whole spirit and soul and body be preserved blameless unto the coming of our Lord Jesus Christ. Faithful is he that calleth you, who also will do it.
-I Thessalonians 5:23-24

Often we are able to hear the voice speaking softly in our hearts; it speaks very softly. We must obey the voice and leave off something which that voice has told us. Also sometimes it tells us to preach or it tells us to witness or it says . . . "Go . . . here . . . or there." . . . as it told Philip, "Approach this chariot."

Thus that voice is that of the Holy Spirit and we must obey it; but when we refuse to obey that voice, at that time, immediately we dry up in our hearts and the blessing will go.

4) Testify.

If we have been given that power, we must use it. If a person has the strength of the body, and he sits all the time and doesn't do a thing and doesn't go about, he becomes a cripple. If we have been given something from God . . . many blessings, and we give it out before others, we increasingly receive other blessings which surpass the others. I imagine that those who have found that blessing know, that when they stand and testify or preach, at exactly that time that they are standing, they receive such blessing as flows like a river.

Let us follow holiness in our hearts so then when Jesus comes, we will not fear to come up into His presence. Let us seek for it more than for riches, let us desire it more than gold. He who wrote Hebrews said that he who is not holy shall not see the King God. If we remain in that power we shall remain holy . . . and we shall be happy to meet with our Savior when He shall come.

Lazaro Nitunga

Lazaro Ntunga